GW01393178

A Phantasy and Other Prose Poems

Clark Ashton Smith

DODO PRESS

CONTENTS

A Phantasy

I have dreamt of an unknown land-a land remote in ulterior time, and alien space not ascertainable; the desert of a long-completed past, upon which has settled the bleak irrevocable silence of infinitude; where all is ruined save the stone of tombs and cenotaphs: and where the sole peoples are the kingless, uncounted tribes of the subterranean dead.

Above this land of my dream, citied with tombs and cenotaphs, a red and smouldering sun maintains a spectral day, in alternation with an ashen moon through the black ether where the stars have long since perished. And through the hush of the consummation of time, above the riven monuments and crumbled records of alien history, flit in the final twilight the mysterious wings of seraphim, sent to fulfill ineffable errands, or confer with demons of the abyss: and black, gigantic angels, newly returned form missions of destruction, pause amid the sepulchers to sift from their gloomy and tremendous vans the pale ashes of annihilated stars.

From the Crypts of Memory

Aeons of aeons ago, in an epoch whose marvelous worlds have crumbled, and whose mighty suns are less than shadow, I dwelt in a star whose course, decadent from the high, irremeable heavens of the past, was even then verging upon the abyss in which, said astronomers, its immemorial cycle should find a dark and disastrous close.

Ah, strange was that gulf-forgotten star - how stranger than any dreams of dreamers in the spheres of to-day, or than any vision that hath soared upon visionaries, in their retrospection of the sideral past! There, through cycles of history whose piled and bronze-writ records were hopeless of tabulation, the dead had come to outnumber infinitely the living. And built of a stone that was indestructible save in the furnace of suns, their cities rose beside those of the living like the prodigious metropoli of Titans, with walls that overgloom the vicinal villages. And over all was the black funereal vault of the cryptic heavens-a dome ol infinite shadows, where the dismal sun, suspended like a sole, enormous lamp, failed to illumine, and drawing back its fires from the face of the irresolvable a baffled and despairing beam on the vague remote horizons, and shrouded vistas illimitable of the visionary land.

We were a sombre, secret, many-sorrowed people-we who dwelt beneath that sky of eternal twilight, pierced by the towering tombs and obelisks of the past. In our blood was the chill of the ancient night of time; and our pulses flagged with a creeping prescience of the lentor of Lethe. Over our courts and fields, like invisible sluggish vampires born of mausoleums, rose and hovered the black hours, with wings that distilled a malefic languor made from the shadowy woe and despair of perished cycles. The very skies were fraught with oppression, and we breathed beneath them as in a sepulcher, forever sealed with all its stagnancies of corruption and slow decay, and darkness impenetrable save to the fretting worm.

Vaguely we lived, and loved as in dreams-the dim and mystic dreams that hover upon the verge of fathomless sleep. We felt for our women, with their pale and spectral beauty, the same desire that the dead may feel for the phantom lilies of Hadean meads. Our days were spent in roaming through the ruins of lone and immemorial cities, whose palaces of fretted copper, and streets that ran between lines of carven golden obelisks, lay dim and ghastly with the dead light, or were drowned forever in seas of stagnant shadow; cities whose vast and iron-builded fanes preserved their gloom of primordial mystery and awe, from which the simulacra of century-forgotten gods looked forth with unalterable eyes to the hopeless heavens, and saw the ulterior night, the ultimate oblivion. Languidly we kept our gardens, whose grey lilies concealed a necromantic perfume, that had power to evoke for us the dead and spectral dreams of the past. Or, wandering through ashen fields of perennial autumn, we sought the rare and mystic immorteles, with sombre leaves and pallid petals, that bloomed beneath willows of wan and veil-like foliage: or swept with a sweet and nepenthe-laden dew by the flowing silence of Acherontic waters.

And one by one we died and were lost in the dust of accumulated time. We knew the years as a passing of shadows, and death itself as the yielding of twilight unto night.

The Memnons of the Night

Ringed with a bronze horizon, which, at a point immensely remote, seems welded with the blue brilliance of a sky of steel, they oppose the black splendour of their porphyritic forms to the sun's insuperable gaze. Reared in the morning twilight of primeval time, by a race whose towering tombs and cities are one with the dust of their builders in the slow lapse of the desert, they abide to face the terrible latter dawns, that move abroad in a starkness of fire, consuming the veils of night on the vast and Sphinx-like desolations. Level with the light, their tenebrific brows preserve a pride as of Titan kings. In their lidless implacable eyes of staring stone, is the petrified despair of those who have gazed too long on the infinite.

Mute as the mountains from whose iron matrix they were hewn, their mouths have never acknowledged the sovereignty of the suns, that pass in triumphal flame from horizon unto horizon of the prostrate land. Only at eve, when the west is a brazen furnace, and the far-off mountains smoulder like ruddy gold in the depth of the heated heavens — only at eve, when the east grows infinite and vague, and the shadows of the waste are one with the increasing shadow of night then, and then only, from their sullen throats of stone, a music rings to the bronze horizon — a strong, a sombre music, strange and sonorous, like the singing of black stars, or a litany of gods that invoke oblivion; a music that thrills the desert to its heart of adamant, and trembles in the granite of forgotten tombs, till the last echoes of its jubilation, terrible as the trumpets of doom, are one with the trumpets of infinity.

Ennui

In the alcove whose curtains are cloth-of-gold, and whose pillars are fluted sapphire, reclines the emperor Chan, on his couch of ebony set with opals and rubies, and cushioned with the furs of unknown and gorgeous beasts. With implacable and weary gaze, from beneath unmoving lids that seem carven of purple-veined onyx, he stares at the crystal windows, giving upon the infinite fiery azures of a tropic sky and sea. Oppressive as nightmare, a formless nameless fatigue, heavier than any burden the slaves of the mines must bear, lies forever at his heart: all deliriums of Love and wine, the agonizing ecstasy of drugs, even the deepest and the faintest pulse of delight or pain-all are proven, all are futile, for the outworn but insatiate emperor. Even for a new grief, or a subtler pang than any felt before, he thinks, lying on his bed of ebony, that he would give the silver and vermilion of all his mines, with the crowded caskets, the carcanets and crowns that lie in his most immemorial treasure-vault. Vainly, with the verse of the more inventive poets, the fanciful purple-threaded fabrics of the subtlest looms, the unfamiliar gems and minerals from the uttermost land, the pallid leaves and blood-like petals of a rare and venomous blossom-vainly, with all these, and many stranger devices, wilder, more wonderful diversions, the slaves and sultanas have sought to alleviate the iron hours. One by one he has dismissed them with a weary gesture. And now, in the silence of the heavily curtained alcove, he lies alone, with the canker of ennui at his heart, like the undying mordant worm at the heart of the dead.

Anon, from between the curtains at the head of his couch, a dark and slender hand is slowly extended, clasping a dagger whose blade reflects the gold of the curtain in a thin and stealthily wavering gleam. Slowly, in silence, the dagger is poised, then rises and falls like a splinter of lightning. The emperor cries out, as the blade, piercing his loosely-folded robe, wounds him slightly in the side. In a moment the alcove is filled with armed attendants, who seize and drag forth the would-be assassin-a slave-girl, the princess of a conquered people, who has often, but vainly, implored her freedom from the emperor. Pale, and panting with terror and rage, she faces Chan and the guardsmen, while stories of unimaginable monstrous tortures, of dooms unnamable, crowd upon her memory. But Chan, aroused and startled only for the instant, feels again the insuperable weariness, more strong than anger or fear, and delays to give the expected signal. And then, momentarily moved, perchance, by some ironical emotion, half-akin to gratitude-gratitude for the brief but diverting danger, which has served to alleviate his ennui for a little, he bids them free the princess; and, with a regal courtesy, places about her throat his own necklace of pearls and emeralds, each of which is the cost of an army.

Feb. 26. 1918

The Princess Almeena

From her balcony of pearl, the princess Almeena, clad in a gown of irisated silk, with her long and sable locks unbound, gazes toward the sunset-flooded sea beyond a terrace of green marble that peacocks guard. Below, in the tinted light, fantastic trees whose boles are serpentine, trail their fine and hair-like foliage, that mingles with the moon-shaped leaves of enormous lilies, Rainbow-coloured reeds cluster about the pools and fountains of black water that are rimmed with carven malachite. But these the princess does not heed, but gazes upon the far-off seas, where the golden ichors of the sun have gathered in a vast lake that overflows the horizon. Ere long, a wind from the west, from isles where palm-trees blossom above the purple foam, brings in its breath the odour of unknown flowers, to mingle with the balms of the garden and the sweet suspiration of the princess, who dreams, listening to the wind, that her lover, the captain of the emperor's most redoubtable trireme of war, sailing the sky-blue seas beyond the horizon and the sunset, has breathed in his heart a secret sigh.

The Black Lake

In a land where weirdness and mystery had strongly leagued themselves with eternal desolation, the lake was out-poured at an undiscoverable date of elder aeons, to fill some fathomless gulf far down amid the shadows of snowless, volcanic mountains. No eye, not even the sun's, when he stared vertically upon it for a few hours at midday, seemed able to divine its depths of sullen blackness and unrippled silence. It was for this reason that I found a so singular pleasure in frequently contemplating the strange lake. Sitting for I knew not how long on its bleak basaltic shores, where grew but a few fleshly red orchids, bent above the waters like open and thirsty mouths, I would peer with countless fantastic conjectures and shadowy imaginings, into the alluring mystery of its unknown and inexplorable gulf.

It was at an hour of morning before the sun had surmounted the rough and broken rim of the summits, when I first came, and clomb down through the shadows which filled like some subtler fluid the volcanic basin. Seen at the bottom of the stirless tincture of air and twilight, the lake seemed as dregs of darkness.

Peering for the first time, after the deep and difficult descent, into the so dull and leaden waters, I was at length aware of certain small and scattered gleams of silver, apparently far beneath the surface. And fancying them the metal in some mysterious ledge, or the glints of long-sunken treasure. I bent closer in my eagerness, and finally perceived that what I saw was but the reflection of the stars, which, tho the day was full upon the mountains and the lands without, were yet visible in the depth and darkness of that enshadowed place.

The Caravan

My dreams are like a caravan that departed long ago, with tumult of intrepid banners and spears, and the clamour of bugles and brave, adventurous songs, to seek the horizons of perilous, unknown, barbaric lands and kingdoms immense and vaguely rumoured, with cities beautiful and opulent as the cities of Paradise, and deep, Edenic vales of palm and cinnamon and myrrh, lying beneath skies of primeval azure silence. For traffic in the realms of mystery and wonder, in the marts of scarce-imaginable cities, and metropoli a million leagues away, on the last horizon of romance, my dreams departed, as a caravan with its laden camels. Since then, the years are many, the days have flown as the flocks of southering swallow; unnumbered moons have multiplied in fugitive silver, uncounted suns in irretainable gold. But, alas, the caravan has not returned. Have the swirling sands engulfed them, on a noon of storm when the desert rose like the sea, and rolled its tawny billows on the walled gardens of the green and fragrant lands? Or perished they, devoured by the crimsom demons of thirst, and the ghouls and vultures? Or live they still, as captives in alien dungeons not to be ascertained, or held by a wizard spell in palaces demon-built, and cities baroque and splendid as the cities in a tale from the Thousand and One Nights?

The Demon, the Angel, and Beauty

Of the Demon who standeth or walketh always with me at my left hand, I asked: "Hast thou seen Beauty? Her that meseemeth was the mistress of my soul in Eternity? Her that is now beyond question set over me in Time; even though I behold her not, and, it may be, have never beheld, nor ever shall; her of whose aspect I am ignorant as noon is concerning any star: her of whom as witness and testimony, I have found only the hem of her shadow, or at most, her reflection in a dim and troubled water. Answer, if thou canst, and tell me, is she like pearls, or like stars? Does she resemble most the sunlight that is transparent and unbroken, or the sunlight divided into splendour and iris? Is she the heart of the day, or the soul of the night?"

To which the Demon answered, after, as I thought, a brief space of meditation:

"Concerning this Beauty, I can tell thee but little beyond that which thou knowest. Albeit, in those orbs to which the demons of my rank have admission, there be greater adumbrations of some transcendent Mystery than here, yet have I never seen that Mystery itself, and know not if it be male or female. Aeons ago, when I was young and incautious, when the world was new and bright, and there were more stars than now, I, too, was attracted by this Mystery, and sought after it in all accessible spheres. But failing to find the thing itself, I soon grew wear of embracing its shadows, and took to the pursuit of illusions less insubstantial. Now I am become grey and ashen without and red like old fire within, who was fiery and flame-coloured all through, back in the star-thronged aeons of which I speak: Heed me, for I am as wise, and wary and ancient as the far-travelled and comet-scarred sun; and I am become of the opinion that the thing Beauty itself does not exist, Doubtless the semblance thereof is but a web of shadow and delusion, woven by the crafty hand of God, that He may snare demons and men therewith, for His mirth, and the laughter of His archangels."

The Demon ceased, and took to watching me as usual-obliquely, and with one eye-an eye that is more red than Aldebaran, and inscrutable as the gulfs beyond the Hyades.

Then of the Angel, who walketh or standeth always with me at my right hand, I asked, "Hast thou seen Beauty? Or hast thou heard any assured rumour concerning Beauty?"

To which the Angel answered, after, as I thought, a moment of hesitation:

"As to this Beauty, I can tell thee but little beyond that which thou knowest, Albeit in all the heavens, this Mystery is a topic of the most frequent and sublime speculation among the archangels, and a perennial theme for the more inspired singers and harpists of the cherubim-yea, despite all this, we are greatly ignorant as to its true nature, and substance, and attributes. But sometimes there are mighty adumbrations which cover even the superior seraphim from above the wing-tips, and make unfamiliar twilight in heaven. And sometimes there is an echo which fills the empyrean, and hushes the archangelic harps in the midst of their praising of God. This is often, and these visitations of echo and shadow spread an awe over the assembled Thrones and Splendours and Dominations, which at other times accompanies only the emanence or appearance of God Himself. Thus are we assured as to the reality of this Beauty. And because it remains a mystery to us, to whom naught else is mysterious except God, we conjecture that it is the thing upon which God meditateth, self-obscured and centred, and because of which He hath held Himself immanifest to us for so many aeons: that this is the secret which God keepeth even from the seraphim."

A Dream of Lethe

In the quest of her whom I had lost, I came at length to the shores of Lethe, under the vault of an immense, empty, ebon sky, from which all the stars had vanished one by one. Proceeding I knew not whence, a pale, elusive light as of the waning moon, or the phantasmal phosphorescence of a dead sun, lay dimly and without lustre on the sable stream, and on the black, flowerless meadows. By this light, I saw many wandering souls of men and women, who came, hesitantly or in haste, to drink of the slow unmurmuring waters. But among all these, there were none who departed in haste, and many who stayed to watch, with unseeing eyes, the calm and waveless movement of the stream. At length in the lily-tall and gracile form, and the still, uplifted face of a woman who stood apart from the rest, I saw the one whom I had sought; and, hastening to her side, with a heart wherein old memories sang like a nest of nightingales, was fain to take her by the hand. But in the pale, immutable eyes, and wan, unmoving lips that were raised to mine, I saw no light of memory, nor any tremor of recognition. And knowing now that she had forgotten, I turned away despairingly, and finding the river at my side, was suddenly aware of my ancient thirst for its waters, a thirst I had once thought to satisfy at many diverse springs, but in vain. Stooping hastily, I drank, and rising again, perceived that the light had died or disappeared, and that all the land was like the land of a dreamless slumber, wherein I could no longer distinguish the faces of my companions. Nor was I able to remember any longer why I wished to drink of the waters of oblivion.

The Flower-Devil

In a basin of porphyry, at the summit of a pillar of serpentine, the thing has existed from primeval time, in the garden of the kings that rule an equatorial realm of the planet Saturn. With black foliage, fine and intricate as the web of some enormous spider; with petals of livid rose, and purple like the purple of putrefying flesh; and a stem rising like a swart and hairy wrist from a bulb so old, so encrusted with the growth of centuries that it resembles an urn of stone, the monstrous flower holds dominion over all the garden. In this flower, from the years of oldest legend, an evil demon has dwelt- a demon whose name and whose nativity are known to the superior magicians and mysteriarchs of the kingdom, but to none other. Over the half-animate flowers, the ophidian orchids that coil and sting, the bat-like lilies that open their ribbèd petals by night, and fasten with tiny yellow teeth on the bodies of sleeping dragonflies; the carnivorous cacti that yawn with green lips beneath their beards of poisonous yellow prickles; the plants that palpitate like hearts, the blossoms that pant with a breath of poisonous perfume - over all these, the Flower-Devil is supreme, in its malign immortality, and evil, perverse intelligence- inciting them to strange maleficence, fantastic mischief, even to acts of rebellion against the gardeners, who proceed about their duties with wariness and trepidation, since more than one of them has been bitten, even unto death, by some vicious and venefic flower. In places, the garden has run wild from lack of care on the part of the fearful gardeners, and has become a monstrous tangle of serpentine creepers, and hydra-headed plants, convolved and inter-writhing in lethal hate or venomous love, and horrible as a rout of wrangling vipers and pythons.

And, like his innumerable ancestors before him, the king dares not destroy the Flower, for fear that the devil, driven from its habitation, might seek a new home, and enter into the brain or body of one of the king's subjects-or even the heart of his fairest and gentlest, and most beloved queen!

From a Letter

Will you not join me in Atlantis, where we will go down through streets of blue and yellow marble to the wharves of orichalch, and choose us a galley with a golden Eros for figurehead, and sails of Tyrian sendal? With mariners that knew Odysseus, and beautiful amber-breasted slaves from the mountain-vales of Lemuria, we will lift anchor for the unknown fortunate isles of the outer sea; and, sailing in the wake of an opal sunset, will lose that ancient land in the glaucous twilight, and see from our couch of ivory and satin the rising of unknown stars and perished planets. Perhaps we will not return, but will follow the tropic summer from isle to halcyon isle, across the amaranthine seas of myths and fable. We will eat the lotos, and the fruit of lands whereof Odysseus never dreamt; and drink the pallid wines of faery, grown in a vale of perpetual moonlight. I will find for you a necklace of rosy-tinted pearls, and a necklace of yellow rubies, and crown you with precious corals that have the semblance of sanguine-coloured blossoms. We will roam in the marts of forgotten cities of jasper, and carnelian-builded ports beyond Cathay; and I will buy you a gown of peacock azure damascened with copper and gold and vermilion; and a gown of black samite with runes of orange, woven by fantastic sorcery without the touch of hands, in a dim land of spells and philtres.

The Garden and the Tomb

I know a garden of flowers-flowers lovely and marvellous and multiform as the orchids of far, exotic worlds-as the flowers of manifold petal, whose colours change as if by enchantment in the alternation of the triple suns; flowers like tiger lilies from the garden of Satan; like the paler lilies of Paradise, or the amaranths on whose perfect and immortal beauty the seraphim so often ponder; flowers fierce and splendid like the crimson or golden flowers of fire; flowers bright and cold as the crystal flowers of snow; flowers whereof there is no likeness in any world of any sun; which have no symbol in heaven or in hell.

Alas! in the heart of the garden is a tomb-a tomb so trellised and embowered with vine and blossom, that the sunlight reveals the ghastly gleam of its marble to no careless or incurious scrutiny, But in the night, when all the flowers are still, and their perfumes are faint as the breathing of children in slumber-then, and then only, the serpents bred of corruption crawl from the tomb, and trail the fetor and phosphorescence of their abiding-place from end to end of the garden.

June 9, 1915.

In Cocaigne

It was a windless afternoon of April, beneath skies that were tender as the smile of love, when we went forth, you and I, to seek the fabulous and fortunate realm of Cocaigne. Past leafing oaks with foliage of bronze and chrysolite, through zones of yellow and white and red and purple flowers, like a landscape seen through a prism, we fared with hopeful and tremulous hearts, forgetting all save the dream we had cherished. *** At last we came to the lonely woods, the pines with their depth of balmy, cool, compassionate shadow, which are sacred to the genius of that land. There, for the first time I was bold to take your hand in mine, and led you to a slope where the woodland lilies, with petals of white and yellow ivory, gleamed among the fallen needles. As in a dream, I found that my arms were about you, as in a dream I kissed your yielding lips, and the ardent pallor of your cheeks and throat. Motionless, you clung to me, and a flush arose beneath my kisses like a delicate stain, and lingered softly, Your eyes deepened to my gaze like the brown pools of the forest at evening, and far within them, as in immensity itself, trembled and shone the steadfast stars of your love. As a ship that has wandered beneath stormy suns and disastrous moons, but comes at last to the arms of the shielding harbour, my head lay on the gentle heaving of your delicious breast, and I knew that we had found Cocaigne.

The Lake of Enchanted Silence

It lies with in a land that is only seen by the sun and the moon and the horizon-questing stars. The sky-wrestled mountains, like sentries of Eternity, surround with their immemorial zone of azure-shadowed snows the serenity of the lake's unfathomable dream. They bar therefrom the sounds of the aeons that thunder on the shores of Eternity, and the winds that ring with the rumour of iron years, and shut from all save the azure infinite, and the fires and clouds and shadows of the sky.

The lake is feed with the snows of the mountains, and with silence that flows from the mien of space, and is filled with the blue splendour of the sky. Infinitely finds itself doubled herein.

On the shore of the lake grow the blue and white amaranths of a perennial summer, and there is no life save that of butterflies and the most beautiful birds. He who penetrates this land may drink the silence of the lake, and look upon it till the image of infinity fills imperturbably the depths of a mind that has become as calm and smooth as the waters.

The Litany of the Seven Kisses

I

I kiss thy hands-thy hands. whose fingers are delicate and the pale as the petals of the white lotus.

II

I kiss thy hair, which has the lustre of black jewels, and is darker than Lethe, flowering by midnight through the moonless slumber of poppy-scented lands.

III

I kiss thy brow, which resembles the rising moon in a valley of cedars.

IV

I kiss thy cheeks, where lingers a faint flush, like the reflection of a rose upheld to an urn of alabaster.

V

I kiss thine eyelids, and liken them to the purple veined flowers and close beneath the oppression of a topic evening, in a land where the sunsets are bright as the flames of burning amber.

VI

I kiss thy throat, whose ardent pallor is the pallor of marble warmed by the autumn sun.

VII

I kiss thy mouth, which has the savour and perfume of fruit made moist with spray from a magic fountain, in the secret paradise that we alone shall fine; a paradise whence they that come shall nevermore depart, for the waters thereof are Lethe, and the fruit is the fruit of the tree of Life.

April 13, 1921.

Remoteness

There are days when all the beauty of the world is dim and strange; when the sunlight about me seems to fall on a land remoter than the poles of the moon. The roses in the garden surprise me, like the monstrous orchids of unknown colour, that blossom in planets beyond Aldebaran. And I am startled by the yellow and purple leaves of October, as if the veil of some tremendous and awful mystery were half-withdrawn for the moment. In such hours as these, O heart of my heart, I fear to touch thee, I avoid thy caresses, dreading that thou wilt vanish as a dream at dawn, or that I shall find thee a phantom, the spectre of one who died and was forgotten many thousand years ago, in a far-off land on which the sun no longer shines.

The Shadows

There were many shadows in the palace of Augusthes, About the silver throne that had blackened beneath the invisible passing of ages, they fell from pillar and broken roof and fretted window in ever-shifting multiformity. Seeming the black, fantastic spectres of doom and desolation, they moved through the palace in a gradual, grave, and imperceptible dance, whose music was the change and motion of suns and moons. They were long and slender, like all other shadows, before the early light, and behind the declining sun; squat and intense beneath the desert noontide, and faint with the withered moon; and in the interlunar darkness, they were as myriad tongues hidden behind the shut and silent lips of night.

One came daily to that place of shadows and desolation, and sate upon the silver throne, watching the shadows that were of desolation. King nor slave disputed him there, in the palace whose kings and whose slaves were powerless alike in the intangible dungeon of centuries. The tombs of unnumbered and forgotten monarchs were white upon he yellow desert roundabout. Some had partly rotted away, and showed like the sunken eye-sockets of a skull-blank and lidless beneath the staring heavens; others still retained the undesecrated seal of death, and were as the closed eyes of one lately dead. But he who watched the shadows from the silver throne, heeded not these, nor the fleet wind that dipt to the broken tombs, and emerged shrilly, its unseen hands dark with the dust of kings.

He was a philosopher, from what land there was none to know or ask. Nor was there any to ask what knowledge or delight he sought in the ruined palace, with eyes always upon the moving shadows; nor what were the thoughts that moved through his mind in ghostly unison with them. His eyes were old and sad with meditation and wisdom; and his beard was long and white upon his long white robe.

For many days he came with the dawn, and departed with sunset; and his shadow leaned from the shadow of the throne and moved with the others. But one eve he departed not; and thereafter his shadow was one with the shadow of the Silver throne. Death found and left him there, where he dwindled into dust that was as the dust of slaves or kings.

But the ebb and refluence of shadows went on, in the days that were before the end; ere the aged world, astray with the sun in strange heavens, should be lost in the cosmic darkness, or, under the influence of other and conflicting gravitations, should crumble apart and bare its granite bones to the light of strange suns, and the granite, too, should dissolve, and be as of the dust of slaves and kings. Noon was encircled with darkness, and the depths of palace-dusk were chasmed with sunlight. Change there was none, other than this, for the earth was dead, and stirred not to the tottering feet of Time. And in the expectant silence before the twilight of the sun, the moving shadows seemed but a mockery of change; a meaningless antic phantasmagoria of things that were; an afterfiguring of forgotten time.

And now the sun was darkened slowly in mid-heaven, as by some vast and invisible bulk. And twilight hushed the shadows in the palace of Augusthes, as the world itself swung down toward the long and single shadow of irretrievable oblivion.

The Statue of Silence

I saw a statue, carven I knew not of what substance, nor with what form or feature, because of the manifold draper of black which fell about it as a veil or a pall. Turning to Psyche, who was with me, I said, "O thou who knowest by name and form the eidola of all things, pray tell me what thing is this." And she answered, "The name of it is Silence, but neither man nor god nor demon knoweth the form thereof, nor its entity. The seraphim pause often before it, waiting the day when the shape shall be unveiled, and the gods and demons of the universe are mute in its presence, half-hoping, half-fearing the time when these lips shall speak, and deliver forth one dreameth not what of oracle, or query, or doom, or judgement."

To the Daemon

Tell me many tales, O benign maleficent daemon, but tell me none that I have ever heard or have even dreamt of otherwise than obscurely or infrequently. Nay, tell me not of anything that lies between the bourns of time or the limits of space: for I am a little wear of all recorded years and charted lands; and the isles that are westward of Cathay, and the sunset realms of Ind, are not remote enough to be made the abiding-place of my conceptions; and Atlantis is over-new for my thoughts to sojourn there, and Mu itself has gazed upon the sun in aeons that are too recent,

Tell me many tales, but let them be of things that are past the fore of legend and of which there are no myths in our world or any world adjoining. Tell me, if you will, of the years when the moon was young, with siren-rippled seas and mountains that were zoned with flowers from base to summit; tell me of the planets gray with eld, of the worlds whereon no mortal astronomer has ever looked, and whose mystic heavens and horizons have given pause to visionaries. Tell me of the vaster blossoms within whose cradling chalices a woman could sleep; of the seas of fire that beat on strands of ever-during ice; of perfumes that can give eternal slumber in a breath; of eyeless titans that dwell in Uranus, and beings that wander in the green light of the twin suns of azure and orange. Tell me tales of inconceivable fear and unimaginable love, in orbs whereto our sun is a nameless star, or unto which its rays have never reached.

The Traveller

(Dedicated to V.H.)

"Stranger, where goest thou, in the sad raiment of a pilgrim, with shattered sandals retaining the dustand mire of so many devious ways? With thy brows that alien suns have darkened, and thy hair made whitefrom the cold rime of alien moons? Wanderest thou in search of the cities greater than Rome, with walls of opal and crystal, and fanes more white than the summer clouds, or the foam of hyperboreal seas? Or farest thou to the lands unpeopled and unexplored, to the sunless deserts lit by the baleful and calamitous beacons of volcanoes? Or seekest thou an extremer shore, where the red and monstrous lilies are like a royal pageant, pausing with innumerable flambeaux held aloft on the verge of the waveless waters?"

"Nay, it is none of these that I seek, but forevermore I seek the city and the land of my former home: In the quest thereof I have wandered from the first, immemorable years of my youth till now, and have mingled the dust of many realms, of many highways, in my garments' hem. I have seen the cities greater than Rome, and the fanes more white than the clouds of summer; the lands unpeopled and unexplored, and the land that is thronged by the red and monstrous lilies. Even the far, aerial walls of the cities of mirage, and the saffron meadows of sunset I have seen, but nevermore the city and land of my former home."

"Where lieth the land of thine home? And by what name shall we know it, and distinguish the rumour thereof, among the rumours of many lands?"

"Alas! I know not where it lieth: nor in the broad, black scrolls of geographers, and the charts of old seamen who have sailed to the marge of the seventh sea, is the place thereof recorded. And its name I have never learned, howbeit I have learned the name of empires lying beneath stars to us invisible. In many languages have I spoken, in barbarous tongues unknown to Babel; and I have heard the speech of many men, even of them that inhabit the strangle isles of the sea of fire and the sea of snow. Thunder, and lutes, and battle-drums, the unceasing querulousness of gnats, and the stupendous moaning of the simoon; lyres of ebony damascened with crystal, bells of malachite with golden clappers, the song of exotic birds that sigh like women or sob like fountains; whispers and shoutings of fire, the multitudinous mutter of cities asleep, the manifold tumult of cities at dawn, and the slow and weary murmur of desert-wandering streams-all, all have I herd, but never, in any place, from my tongue, a word or syllable that resembled in the least in the name I would learn."

LaVergne, TN USA
28 February 2011
218203LV00002B/120/P